THE CASE FOR Christmas

THE CASE FOR Christmas

Evidence for the Identity of Jesus

STUDY GUIDE | 4 SESSIONS

LEE STROBEL

WITH BILL BUTTERWORTH

The Case for Christmas Study Guide

This title is also available as a Zondervan ebook.

Requests for information should be addressed to:
Zondervan, *3900 Sparks Dr. SE, Grand Rapids, Michigan 49546*

ISBN 978-0-310-09929-1

First Printing September 2018 / Printed in the United States of America

Contents

How to Use This Guide

Do you have questions about the first Christmas? Then you are in the right place. During the next four weeks, you and your group will look at the story surrounding the birth of Jesus—and how you can know that the events recorded in the Bible are true.

The Case for Christmas video study is designed to be experienced in a group setting such as a Bible study, Sunday school class, or any small group gathering. Each session begins with a brief introduction and opening questions to get you and your group thinking about the topic. You will then watch a video with Lee Strobel and jump into some directed small-group discussion. You will close each session with a time of prayer.

Each person in the group should have his or her own study guide, which includes video teaching notes, group discussion questions, and between-sessions personal studies to help you reflect on the material during the week. You are also encouraged to have a copy of *The Case for Christmas* book, as reading it alongside the curriculum will provide you with deeper insights and make the journey more meaningful.

To get the most out of your group experience, keep the following points in mind. First, the real growth in this study will happen during your small-group time. This is where you will process the content of Lee's message, ask questions, and learn from others as you hear what God is doing in their lives. For this reason, it is important for you to be fully committed to the group and attend each session so you can build trust and rapport with the other members. If you choose to only "go through the motions," or if you refrain from participating, there is a lesser chance you will find what you're looking for during this study.

Second, the goal of your small group is to serve as a place where you can share, learn about God, and build intimacy and friendship with others. For this reason, seek to make your group a "safe place." This means being honest about your thoughts and feelings and listening carefully to everyone else's opinion. Resist the temptation to "fix" someone's problem or correct his or her theology, as that's not the purpose of your small-group time. Also, keep everything your group shares confidential. This will foster a rewarding sense of community in your group and create a place where people can heal, be challenged, and grow spiritually.

In between your group times, you can maximize the impact of the curriculum by completing the personal study activities. This individual study will help you reflect and actively respond to the lesson. You may wish to complete the personal study in one sitting or spread it over a few days (for example, working on it a half hour per day on four different days that week). Note that if you are unable to finish (or even start!) your between-sessions personal study, you should still attend the group study video session. You are still wanted and welcome at the group even if you don't have your "homework" done.

Keep in mind that the videos, discussions, and activities are simply meant to kick-start your imagination, so you will be open to what God wants you to hear through this study. The goal is for you to see the Christmas story in a whole new light and know with confidence that the Gospel accounts of Jesus' birth are accurate and true. This will hopefully prove to be a journey that will stimulate your mind, warm your heart, and satisfy your soul.

Sound good? Then let's get started.

Note: If you are a group leader, there are additional resources provided in the back of this guide to help you lead your group members through the study.

SESSION 1

Setting the Record Straight

• • • • • • • • •

The Son of God became a man to enable men to become sons of God.

–C. S. Lewis, *Mere Christianity*

Introduction

Holidays just bring out the best in us. Whether it's roses and chocolates for Valentine's Day, or baskets of candy for Easter, or flags and fireworks for the Fourth of July, we love the celebratory focus a holiday brings to our lives.

Of course, there's little debate over the best of all holidays. It has to be Christmas. When you close your eyes, you can almost see the forest as you hike to cut down your very own Christmas tree. The scent of fresh pine permeates the air on the way back to the car—and once home, there's the smell of those Christmas cookies in the oven that the kids and grandkids created in the shapes of angels, shepherds, and Christmas trees.

The sounds of Christmas fill the house with the music of the season. You've already lost track of how many times you've heard Bing Crosby sing "White Christmas" or Elvis sing "Blue Christmas" or Mariah Carey sing "All I Want for Christmas Is You." The lights on the newly decorated tree bring a warm glow to the whole house.

As evening falls and the dinner dishes are cleared, it's time for another Christmas tradition—watching those classic Christmas movies. There's a long list of family favorites: *A Christmas Carol*, *Holiday Inn*, *A Christmas Story*, *Miracle on 34th Street*, *Home Alone*, *Elf*, *How the Grinch Stole Christmas*, and *Christmas Vacation* . . . just to name a few.

And let's not forget what many consider the finest Christmas movie ever made—Frank Capra's *It's A Wonderful Life*. You remember that one, don't you? The movie centers on George Bailey, who lives with his wife and children in Bedford Falls. The drama begins when George's Uncle Billy is supposed to deposit $8,000 of George's business receipts into the bank, but Billy loses the money. The town villain, Mr. Potter, finds the cash and realizes it is exactly what he needs to put George out of business. In doing so, he can then take over the town.

George is despondent when he hears about the loss and doesn't know what to do. He believes his life insurance policy could cover the loss, and he concludes that he's worth more to his family dead than alive. As he contemplates suicide, he meets an angel named Clarence, who helps him sort out his issues. Clarence shows George what the world would be like without him in it. George discards the plan for suicide. A happy ending ensues.

There are so many memorable lines in the movie, but one stands out for our purposes. It's a tantalizing theological morsel uttered by the Baileys' little daughter, Zuzu:

> Every time a bell rings, an angel gets his wings.

You don't have to be a learned theologian to sniff out the theological weakness of Zuzu's statement. The connection between bells and angel wings seems flimsy at best. But did you know there are more traditional statements about Christmas—the first Christmas—that are equally suspect? We will look at a few of those in this opening session.

Before You Watch

Pair up with another group member, ideally someone you don't know that well, and briefly talk about the following questions:

- What's your favorite Christmas movie? How about a favorite character? Is there a favorite memory you can share of a time when you watched this movie with your family or friends?
- What is your family's tradition as it relates to the opening of presents? Does your family open their gifts on Christmas Eve or on Christmas morning?
- Do you have a nativity scene that you display during this time of year? What would that scene look like without the stable or the wise men? (It would make the scene look a bit different and less familiar, wouldn't you agree?)

Video Teaching

Play the video segment for session one. As you watch, use the following outline to record any thoughts or concepts that stand out to you.

Notes

It would have been unthinkable in the first century for anyone to turn away a pregnant Jewish woman seeking shelter. The person who turned her away would be ostracized.

Luke specifically chose the Greek word *katalyma* in the account of Jesus' birth, which is best translated as "guest room." In fact, the *New International Version* translates Luke 2:7 as saying Mary placed Jesus in a manger "because there was no *guest room* available for them."

Luke says the time for Jesus to be born came *"while they were there"* in Bethlehem. Luke doesn't portray this as an emergency situation that arose as they approached the village.

What about the idea that Mary gave birth in a cave? Actually, the Gospels don't mention a cave at all. In fact, the idea of a cave can be traced back to Christian apologist Justin Martyr, who was writing much later—during the middle of the second century.

It's a legitimate question to ask whether we can trust the Gospel accounts. How do we know they are reliable? Can we be sure they are trustworthy when they describe the birth, the teachings, the death, and—ultimately—the resurrection of Jesus? Yes, for two reasons:

> First, they were written a lot closer to the events they describe than some critics claim.

> Second, archaeology has consistently affirmed the biblical record—to the point where Luke has been described by scholars as a first-rate historian.

We need to take seriously the historical record of the birth of Jesus. Because it's true, Christmas cannot be ignored. In the end, the child in the manger deserves our allegiance and our worship.

Group Discussion

Once the video has concluded, break into small groups for a time of discussion. Ideally, the group should be no less than four people and no more than six. Don't be shy—grab your chair and circle up! Find someone who will become your partner over the next few weeks. If you're married and your spouse is in the group, you've got the option of choosing him or her, or you may opt for someone completely different. If not your spouse, it's best for women to choose another woman and men to choose another man. Get your new partner's cell phone number and email so you can connect during the week.

1. Have you ever heard the teaching that Jesus wasn't refused a room at an "inn"? What struck you as the most significant point as that myth was debunked?

2. One scholar suggests Mary and Joseph could have been in Bethlehem "five minutes or five weeks" before the baby Jesus was born, emphasizing the point that there wasn't necessarily any panic. Does that differ from how you have heard the Christmas story? Does it make a difference to you? Share your impressions with the group.

3. What are your thoughts about the reliability of Matthew, Mark, Luke, and John? Do you view their Gospel accounts as trustworthy, or do you have some questions and/or doubts? (It's okay if you do, because that's one of the reasons why you're meeting together this Christmas season. Share your answers honestly with your group.)

4. What other questions have you had about the reliability of Jesus' birth story as told in the Bible? How did this week's teaching help address these concerns? What other questions do you still have at this point that you want to express to the group?

Closing Prayer

Conclude your group discussion time with a few minutes for prayer. Nothing will bring your group together quicker than knowing you have brothers and sisters who care enough about issues you raise to bring them before the Lord for his answers and his direction.

SESSION 1

Between-Sessions Personal Study

Reflect on the content you've covered this week by engaging in any or all of the following between-sessions personal study. The time you invest will be well spent, so let God use it to draw you closer to him. At your next meeting, share with your group any key points or insights that stood out to you as you spent this time with the Lord.

Study God's Word

To investigate the true story of the first Christmas, it will be worth your time to dig deeper into the original accounts, found in Matthew and Luke. For your study this week, concentrate on Matthew's version. Read the following story of the birth of Jesus:

> This is how the birth of Jesus the Messiah came about: His mother Mary was pledged to be married to Joseph, but before they came together, she was found to be pregnant through the

Holy Spirit. Because Joseph her husband was faithful to the law, and yet did not want to expose her to public disgrace, he had in mind to divorce her quietly.

But after he had considered this, an angel of the Lord appeared to him in a dream and said, "Joseph son of David, do not be afraid to take Mary home as your wife, because what is conceived in her is from the Holy Spirit. She will give birth to a son, and you are to give him the name Jesus, because he will save his people from their sins."

All this took place to fulfill what the Lord had said through the prophet: "The virgin will conceive and give birth to a son, and they will call him Immanuel" (which means "God with us").

When Joseph woke up, he did what the angel of the Lord had commanded him and took Mary home as his wife. But he did not consummate their marriage until she gave birth to a son. And he gave him the name Jesus.

After Jesus was born in Bethlehem in Judea, during the time of King Herod, Magi from the east came to Jerusalem and asked, "Where is the one who has been born king of the Jews? We saw his star when it rose and have come to worship him."

When King Herod heard this he was disturbed, and all Jerusalem with him. When he had called together all the people's chief priests and teachers of the law, he asked them where the Messiah was to be born. "In Bethlehem in Judea," they replied, "for this is what the prophet has written:

"'But you, Bethlehem, in the land of Judah,
are by no means least among the rulers of Judah;
for out of you will come a ruler
who will shepherd my people Israel.'"

Then Herod called the Magi secretly and found out from them the exact time the star had appeared. He sent them to Bethlehem and said, "Go and search carefully for the child. As soon as you find him, report to me, so that I too may go and worship him."

After they had heard the king, they went on their way, and the star they had seen when it rose went ahead of them until it stopped over the place where the child was. When they saw the star, they were overjoyed. On coming to the house, they saw the child with his mother Mary, and they bowed down and worshiped him. Then they opened their treasures and presented him with gifts of gold, frankincense and myrrh. And having been warned in a dream not to go back to Herod, they returned to their country by another route.

Matthew 1:18–2:12

As you review what the group covered together during the teaching time, what stands out in this passage that you didn't notice previously?

Look back through the text and circle the words you consider to be key. (Limit the number of these key words to twenty.) Write these words in the left-hand column in the table on page 22. In the center column, write down a brief answer to the question, *Why do I consider this word to be key to the text?* Then take those key words and do your best at defining them in the right-hand column. Use a different word than what was recorded in the text.

Key Word	Why Is It Key?	Word Definition

Put It into Practice

Take some time this week to think about how the material you are covering with your group can make a difference in the way you live your life. In the New Testament book of James, the author implores us to be *doers* of the God's Word and not *hearers* only. The real test of what is important to us is how well we integrate it into our lives.

You can trust the accuracy of the Gospel accounts—thus you can trust the accuracy of the Bible. What difference does that make in the way you live your life?

How does trusting the Bible affect your home life? How does it affect your work life?

How about your friendships? What does it mean in your personal life?

What is the biggest truth you learned this week? Write it down.

What are two more concepts that emerged from your study this week?

How has your time with the group changed the way you view the story of the first Christmas?

How did you think about it before? How do you think about it now?

Make contact with the partner you selected at the meeting either through a text or, better yet, a phone call. Check in to see how he or she is doing:

- Is the person enjoying the study? Why or why not?
- Is there any frustration or confusion that he or she can verbalize?
- How does trusting the Bible make a difference in the way that person is living his or her life?
- Is there anything you can do to be of help to them between now and the next time the entire group gets together?

Talk to your partner about the answers to the previous questions—the big truths you've come away with as a result of the study and how the group experience has made an impact on you thus far.

CLOSING REFLECTION

The *Chicago Tribune* newsroom was eerily quiet on the day before Christmas. As I sat at my desk with little to do, my mind kept wandering back to a family I had encountered a month earlier while I was working on a series of articles about Chicago's neediest people.

The Delgados—sixty-year-old Perfecta and her granddaughters Lydia and Jenny—had been burned out of their roach-infested tenement and were now living in a tiny two-room apartment on the West Side. As I walked in, I couldn't believe how empty it was. There was no furniture, no rugs, nothing on the walls—only a small kitchen table and a handful of rice. That's it. They were virtually devoid of possessions.

In fact, eleven-year-old Lydia and thirteen-year-old Jenny owned only one short-sleeved dress each, plus one thin, gray sweater between them. When they walked the half-mile to school through the biting cold, Lydia would wear the sweater for part of the distance and then hand it to her shivering sister, who would wear it the rest of the way.

But despite their poverty and the painful arthritis that kept Perfecta from working, she still talked confidently about her faith in Jesus. She was convinced he had not abandoned them. I never sensed despair or self-pity in her home; instead, there was a gentle feeling of hope and peace.

I wrote an article about the Delgados and then quickly moved on to more exciting assignments. But as I sat at my desk on Christmas Eve, I continued to wrestle with the irony of the situation: here was a family that had nothing but faith and yet seemed happy, while I had everything I needed materially but lacked faith—and inside I felt as empty and barren as their apartment.

I walked over to the city desk to sign out a car. It was a slow news day with nothing of consequence going on. My boss could call me if something were to happen. In the meantime, I decided to drive over to West Homer Street and see how the Delgados were doing.

When Jenny opened the door, I could not believe my eyes. *Tribune* readers had responded to my article by showering the Delgados with a treasure trove of gifts—roomfuls of furniture, appliances, and rugs; a lavish Christmas tree with piles of presents underneath; carton upon bulging carton of food;

and a dazzling selection of clothing, including dozens of warm winter coats, scarves, and gloves. On top of that, they donated thousands of dollars in cash.

But as surprised as I was by this outpouring, I was even more astonished by what my visit was interrupting; Perfecta and her granddaughters were getting ready to give away much of their newfound wealth. When I asked Perfecta why, she replied in halting English: "Our neighbors are still in need. We cannot have plenty when they have nothing. This is what Jesus would want us to do."

That blew me away! If I had been in their position at that time in my life, I would have been hoarding everything. I asked Perfecta what she thought about the generosity of the people who had sent all these goodies, and again her response amazed me.

"This is wonderful; this is very good," she said, gesturing towards the largess. "We did nothing to deserve this—it's a gift from God. But," she added, "it is not his greatest gift. No, we celebrate that tomorrow. That is Jesus."

To her, this child in the manger was the undeserved gift that meant everything—more than material possessions, more than comfort, more than security. And at that moment, something inside of me wanted desperately to know this Jesus—because, in a sense, I saw him in Perfecta and her granddaughters.

I am hoping and praying you are going to see Jesus over the next four weeks. He won't force himself into your life, but he will definitely make himself available to you. There is no better Christmas gift than the gift of life offered to you by that little baby in the manger.

–Lee Strobel, from The Case for Christmas

SESSION 2

Beneath the Fake News

• • • • • • • • •

[Christ] was born of a virgin, that we might be born of God. He took our flesh, that He might give us His Spirit. He lay in the manger that we might lie in paradise.

–Thomas Watson, *A Body of Divinity*

Introduction

If you are a connoisseur of classic Christmas movies, this brief slice of dialogue should alert you right away to a movie many of us have grown to love:

> **Ralphie:** I want an official Red Ryder, carbine action, two-hundred shot range model air rifle!
> **Mother:** No, you'll shoot your eye out.

Yes, it's the heartwarming tale of Ralphie, star of *A Christmas Story.* Based on the writings of Jean Shepherd, the movie follows Ralphie Parker and his little brother, Randy, as they brave a 1940s snowy winter in the fictional town of Hohman, Indiana. The story recalls a quieter time in America, before television, when families would gather around a large piece of wooden furniture known as a "radio" and listen to serialized episodes of such shows as *The Adventures of Little Orphan Annie* and *The Lone Ranger.*

This Christmas movie has everything. There's a bully. There's a cranky dad. There's a mom who is kind and understanding. There's a lamp in the shape of a leg, a schoolmate who sticks his tongue to a frozen flagpole, and a furnace that breaks down, much to Dad's dismay. But the driving force of the movie is young Ralphie's not-so-secret desire to have Santa Claus bring him that Red Ryder BB gun. He dreams about it—and schemes about it.

Most agree it's the final act of the movie, the celebration of Christmas morning, that represents the high point of the movie.

The boys run down the steps early to discover loads of gifts that Santa has left under the tree. They unwrap them with reckless abandon and unfettered joy. But that unfettered joy suddenly becomes fettered when Ralphie unwraps an unwanted gift from Aunt Clara—a pair of pajamas that looks like a pink bunny rabbit.

When it appears all the gifts have been opened, Dad and Ralphie reflect on the morning. The boy wants to appear grateful, but the gift he most wanted was not among his presents. *Spoiler alert:* It ends up that cranky Dad has a big heart after all. He presents his son with the precious BB gun the boy so desperately wanted.

Many of us can relate to the scenes in *A Christmas Story* because it replicates much of what life was like when we were growing up. Regardless of our age or in what era we grew up, there have always been bullies, bunny-pajama presents, and bighearted fathers with cranky exteriors. The movie is successful because it works off a good story—and a good story *always* connects with people. But there's a difference between *truth* and *story.*

In the account of the birth of Jesus, the Gospels agree that Jesus was born of a *virgin.* Can that be true? Or is it—as many critics have claimed—just a myth, a good story? Today, we will dig in to this part of the Christmas narrative and see what we can discover.

Before You Watch

Pair up with a different group member this week and talk about the following questions:

- Ralphie wanted a BB gun more than anything. What gift did you long for as a child? Did you ever receive it? Was it as amazing as you thought it would be?

- What's the most bizarre Christmas present you've ever received? Was it from a crazy relative? A coworker? What did you end up doing with the gift?
- Have you ever received a heartwarming gift from a person best described as having a "cranky exterior"? Describe how it happened.

Video Teaching

Play the video segment for session two. As you watch, use the following outline to record any thoughts or concepts that stand out to you.

Notes

Critics say there were stories of an earlier mythological god named Mithras long before Jesus was born—who was born of a virgin, in a cave, on December 25, had twelve disciples, sacrificed himself for world peace, was buried in a tomb, and rose again three days later. Sound familiar?

Mithras actually wasn't born of a virgin. Instead, the myth says he emerged fully grown out of a rock—and he was wearing a hat!

It is true Mithras might have been born on December 25. But so what? The Gospels don't tell us when Jesus was born.

There is no clear evidence that pagan sources used the word *virgin* as referring to the mothers of heroes, mythical or historical, who were represented as being begotten by the gods.

Many of the supposed virgin-birth stories don't occur until *after* Christianity—so if there was any borrowing, it would be in the other direction. Even if some stories did come before Jesus, it doesn't mean they influenced Christianity.

The myths and legends bear no resemblance to the incarnation of Jesus. They are generally mythological tales about gods desiring mortal women, who give birth to half-human, half-divine heroes who have the same weaknesses and sins as we do.

No search for parallels has given a truly satisfactory explanation of how early Christians happened upon the idea of a virginal conception—unless, of course, it really took place.

The reports of Jesus' birth, teachings, death, and resurrection appear in a historical context, are based on eyewitness accounts, and are recorded virtually immediately after his life.

Group Discussion

Once the video has concluded, break up into small groups for a time of discussion. Ideally, this should be the group you formed during the last session, but you can create a new group of four to six people if necessary. Don't be shy—grab your chair and circle up!

1. How much did you know about Mithras or the other legends mentioned prior to the teaching you just saw? What do you think about the similarities between the virgin birth of Jesus and some of the mythological concepts that seem similar?

2. Read aloud Hebrews 4:15. Most of the mythological tales on which critics say Jesus' birth story is based involve a hero who is half god/half man, but he struggles with sin and weakness. How does this differ from what the Bible teaches about Jesus?

3. Why is it advantageous to know that the reports of the virgin birth were recorded virtually immediately after Jesus' resurrection and ascension? How does that lend credibility to the claim that Jesus was born of a virgin?

4. What questions have you had in the past about the truth of the virgin birth? How has this week's teaching helped to illuminate these questions? What other questions do you still have at this point that you want to discuss with the group?

Closing Prayer

Conclude your group discussion time with a few minutes for prayer. Start by having everyone share how they are doing in regard to the issues you began praying about last week, and then continue to pray for those needs. Share any new requests that you would like the group members to pray about during this week.

SESSION 2

Between-Sessions Personal Study

Reflect on the content you've covered this week by engaging in any or all of the following between-sessions personal study. The time you invest will be well spent, so let God use it to draw you closer to him. At your next meeting, share with your group any key points or insights that stood out to you as you spent this time with the Lord.

Study God's Word

Last week, you investigated Matthew's account of the first Christmas. But there is one other Gospel writer who records the story. Read the following recorded by Luke:

> In those days Caesar Augustus issued a decree that a census should be taken of the entire Roman world. (This was the first census that took place while Quirinius was governor of Syria.) And everyone went to their own town to register.

So Joseph also went up from the town of Nazareth in Galilee to Judea, to Bethlehem the town of David, because he belonged to the house and line of David. He went there to register with Mary, who was pledged to be married to him and was expecting a child. While they were there, the time came for the baby to be born, and she gave birth to her firstborn, a son. She wrapped him in cloths and placed him in a manger, because there was no guest room available for them.

And there were shepherds living out in the fields nearby, keeping watch over their flocks at night. An angel of the Lord appeared to them, and the glory of the Lord shone around them, and they were terrified. But the angel said to them, "Do not be afraid. I bring you good news that will cause great joy for all the people. Today in the town of David a Savior has been born to you; he is the Messiah, the Lord. This will be a sign to you: You will find a baby wrapped in cloths and lying in a manger."

Suddenly a great company of the heavenly host appeared with the angel, praising God and saying,

"Glory to God in the highest heaven,
and on earth peace to those on whom his favor rests."

When the angels had left them and gone into heaven, the shepherds said to one another, "Let's go to Bethlehem and see this thing that has happened, which the Lord has told us about."

So they hurried off and found Mary and Joseph, and the baby, who was lying in the manger. When they had seen him, they spread the word concerning what had been told them about this child, and all who heard it were amazed at what the shepherds said to them. But Mary treasured up all these things and pondered them in her heart. The shepherds returned, glorifying and praising God for all the things they had heard and seen, which were just as they had been told.

On the eighth day, when it was time to circumcise the child, he was named Jesus, the name the angel had given him before he was conceived.

Luke 2:1–21

In what ways are the Matthew account and the Luke account similar? Write down five ways.

How are they different from each other? Write down five observations that are unique to Matthew and five that are unique to Luke.

Unique to Matthew	Unique to Luke

Think back over what you and the group have studied during the past two sessions. In the left-hand column of the table below, write down a few points that really stood out to you in terms of new information you've learned. In the right-hand column, try to pinpoint a verse or two that references that teaching (see the example provided).

Truth from the Text	Reference
It wasn't an "inn"—it was a guest room	Luke 2:7

The beauty of the Scripture is that it is literally the Word of God speaking to you personally. Much of your personal understanding of the Word will come from your interaction with it—you not only *observe* what the Bible says, but you also *discover* its meaning and then *apply* it to your life. Try your hand today at application by paraphrasing the two accounts of Jesus' birth. This refers to taking a text and writing it out *in your own words*. By doing this, you emphasize what stands out to you in the text and reframe it in a personal way.

Paraphrase the birth of Christ as found in Matthew:

Paraphrase the birth of Christ as found in Luke:

Congratulations—that was a big assignment! Did you find yourself feeling closer to the accounts as you rewrote them in your own words? In what ways?

Was there a point in the exercise where you felt the Lord speaking to you in a personal way? If so, what was he saying to you?

Put a "ribbon on this package" by writing down a few statements that summarize how it felt to interact with these two texts in a personal way. Weave in some of the lessons you've been learning with your group, along with the insights you are gleaning personally.

Put It into Practice

Take some time this week to think about how the material you are covering with your group can make a difference in the way you live your life. Are you beginning to have a new appreciation for the true meaning of Christmas? There's nothing wrong with all the hoopla accompanying December 25th, but there's a more significant meaning. Take a few minutes to write down some of what you are feeling right now. Use the following prompts to help get your thoughts out of your head and onto the page.

I used to think of Christmas as . . .

But now I think of Christmas as . . .

If someone said the virgin birth was just a myth, I would share this information . . .

Here are some changes I plan to make in the way I celebrate Christmas . . .

Take time to check in with your partner. Share the biggest takeaway you've received since the two of you attended the last group meeting. Ask that person about the biggest takeaway he or she has had so far in the study. Check into any prayer requests or concerns that may have developed since you last communicated.

CLOSING REFLECTION

As a teenager growing up on Long Island, Michael Brown's insatiable appetite for illicit drugs earned him the nicknames "Iron Man" and "Drug Bear." By the age of fifteen, the aspiring rock and roll drummer was shooting heroin and had burglarized some homes and even a doctor's office for amusement—an incongruous lifestyle for the son of a senior lawyer of the New York Supreme Court.

He grew up in a Jewish family but was uninterested in spiritual matters. When he was bar mitzvahed at the age of thirteen, he was given a Hebrew passage to memorize—but nobody ever translated it for him and he never bothered to ask anyone what the words meant. For him, it was all a meaningless ritual.

In 1971, the two other members of his band began attending a local church in pursuit of two girls related to the pastor. Little by little, they began to be influenced by the gospel. Upset at the changes in their lives, Brown decided to visit the church in an effort to extricate them. One of the girls, aware of his reputation, wrote in her diary that night: "Anti-Christ comes to church."

Unexpectedly, in the months that followed, Brown discovered a new emotion: a gnawing sense of regret and conviction over his rebellious and drug-saturated behavior. He ended up in many discussions with Christians about spirituality. On November 12, 1971, when the pastor asked if anyone wanted to receive Jesus as their Savior, Brown walked the aisle—not because he really wanted to become a Christian, but so that he could give the congregation a thrill. After all, he was sure they regarded him as the worst of sinners.

Then something even more unexpected happened: as he repeated the words of the pastor in a prayer of repentance and faith, he found himself suddenly believing the message of Christ. It wasn't until five weeks later that he permanently abandoned drugs and yielded his life to Christ.

Brown pursued years of education that ultimately led to a master's degree as well as a doctorate in Near Eastern Languages and Literatures from New York University. His practice of tackling the most powerful arguments of critics has helped him develop into one of America's best-known defenders of Jesus the Messiah.

I interviewed him, and as it came to a close, I asked, "Who's the real Jesus to you?"

Brown glanced off to the side, collecting his thoughts, and then looked back at me. "He's the Messiah of Israel and the Savior of the world. He's the one whom I owe my life and through him I've come to know God. He is the one who provided me complete forgiveness of sins, who loved me when I was a miserable, ungrateful, rebellious, proud wretch. He put a new heart and a new spirit within me. He turned my life around and gave it meaning.

"And he's the only hope for the world."

–*Lee Strobel, from* In Defense of Jesus

SESSION 3

A Mind-Boggling Proposition

• • • • • • • • •

I believe in God, the Father Almighty, creator of heaven and earth. I believe in Jesus Christ, his only Son, our Lord, who was conceived by the Holy Spirit, born of the Virgin Mary, suffered under Pontius Pilate, was crucified, died, and was buried; he descended to the dead.

–The Apostles' Creed

Introduction

There are some Christmas movies that can inspire you. There are some Christmas movies that can make you think. And then there are some Christmas movies that are just plain silly.

One Christmas classic released in 1989 certainly falls into this category—*Christmas Vacation*. It's a screwball comedy written by John Hughes about a dad named Clark Griswold (played by actor Chevy Chase) who leads his wife, Ellen, and his two children, Audrey and Rusty, through a litany of Christmas traditions—each of them ending in destruction.

The film covers all the Christmas movie bases. There's a "shopping for gifts" scene. There's an "extended family shows up unexpectedly" scene, bringing along their corresponding cornucopia of dysfunction. There's a "Christmas Eve dinner is a disaster" scene. There's a running gag in the movie that has Clark attaching 25,000 lights to the exterior of the house. One scene has Clark taking his family to the forest to find the "perfect" Christmas tree:

Clark: You see, kids, this is what our forefathers did.
Audrey: I can't feel my legs.
Clark: They walked out into the woods, they picked out that special tree, and they cut it down with their bare hands.
Audrey: Mom, I can't feel my hips.
Ellen: Clark . . . Audrey's frozen . . .
Clark: It's all part of the experience, honey.

Clark wants this Christmas to be the best ever, but everything ends in disaster. The twenty-pound turkey is left in the oven too long. The uncle sets the "perfect Christmas tree" on fire. Clark cuts down another one from his yard, but it contains a squirrel stowaway. The 25,000 lights won't shine at first when he flips the switch. The big Christmas bonus he was expecting doesn't materialize—in its place is a membership in the "Jelly of the Month Club." Before the movie concludes, there are appearances by the cops, a SWAT team, and Santa and his exploding reindeer. But, as in most comedy farces, it all works out for the Griswolds.

Of course, the movie pushes the bounds of reality. It would be impossible for the exterior of the turkey to look so pristine if the interior was all dried out. The tree that Clark picks out, a Douglas fir, isn't native to Illinois, where the Griswolds supposedly live. The number of Christmas lights Clark puts on his house would require an estimated 157.5 *kilowatts* to run, which would short out the home's main breaker. And had Clark been able to get around that problem, the heat from all those lights would have likely set the roof on fire.

When some people look at the events of Jesus' birth, they often come to the same conclusion. As we saw last week, many critics claim all the stories about Jesus' entrance into this world are based on old legends, myths, and fairy tales. For them, the visit of the magi, the angels, and the star over Bethlehem push the bounds of reality—and the concept of God becoming flesh and being born of a virgin is simply too mind-boggling to be believed.

Today, we will continue to investigate the Christmas story and unwrap this dilemma known as the virgin birth of Christ. We will look at where the evidence points and see if we can truly have confidence that what the Bible says about these events is true.

Before You Watch

Team up with another group member and answer the following questions:

- Are you into decorating your home for Christmas? If so, how elaborate are your decorations?
- What's your favorite part about Christmas dinner? Why?
- Where's the most unusual place you've ever spent Christmas? How did it happen that you were there?

Video Teaching

Play the video segment for session three. As you watch, use the following outline to record any thoughts or concepts that stand out to you.

Notes

God becoming man, spirit taking on flesh, the infinite becoming finite, the eternal becoming time-bound—it's a mind-boggling proposition. And the virgin birth is at the center of it all.

The virgin conception of Jesus is clearly taught in Scripture (see Matthew 1:18; Luke 1:34–35).

Why is the virgin birth important theologically? Two reasons:

> First, it makes it possible for Jesus to be both fully God and fully man, which is a foundational biblical claim about him.

> Second, it makes it possible for Christ to be born without original sin. All other people have inherited a corrupt moral nature, thanks to our first father, Adam.

Some critics maintain the virgin birth is a story invented by Christians many years after Jesus' death as a way to elevate his status. But the reports of the virgin birth are quite early—in fact, within the first generation of Christians.

"In the beginning God created the heavens and the earth" (Genesis 1:1). If we believe in a God who created the universe, then for him to create a *Y* chromosome would be child's play.

This dual nature of Jesus—his humanity and his divinity—is important:

Because of his *humanity*, he can relate to our situation.

Because of his *divinity*, he can give us supernatural wisdom, offer the power of God to help us, perform powerful miracles and wonders, and open up the gates of heaven.

Group Discussion

Once the video has concluded, break up into small groups for a time of discussion. Ideally, this should be the group with whom you've spent the previous two sessions—and by now you should be more comfortable with one another. Circle up and get right down to it!

1. What are some reasons why the virgin birth is important to Christian theology?

Human - Mary
Divine - Holy Spirit

2. Why is it important that Jesus was born fully *divine*? Why is it important that Jesus was born fully *human*?

3. Why would critics say the disciples made up the story of the virgin birth? Is there any advantage to the first-century believers in propagating a lie? For them, would creating a fiction instead of relating the truth really elevate who Jesus was?

4. Read aloud John 1:1. What does that verse say to you? Can you think of other verses from John's Gospel that refer to Jesus as God in one way or another? What other questions do you have about Jesus' divinity that you want to discuss with the group?

ISAIAH - foretold
Virgen Birth

Closing Prayer

Take some time to pair up with your partner. How is he or she doing with this study? Does your partner have more questions than when you began? What are some ways you could help? Keeping this season of gift-gifting in mind, what are two or three things you can tell the person you respect about him or her—things in which the person is gifted? Close by praying together as a group. Be sure to inquire about any new requests that might have surfaced since last session and continue to pray for the needs already before you.

1. Whatever begins to exist has a cause
2. Scientists agree our universe begain in past
3. Must be a cause behind universe

SESSION 3

Between-Sessions Personal Study

Reflect on the content you've covered this week by engaging in any or all of the following between-sessions personal study. The time you invest will be well spent, so let God use it to draw you closer to him. At your next meeting, share with your group any key points or insights that stood out to you as you spent this time with the Lord.

Study God's Word

Of the four Gospels, it is the Gospel of John that has the strongest focus on the deity of Christ. Near the end of the book, John answers the all-important question, "Why did I write this book, anyway?" His answer:

> Jesus performed many other signs in the presence of his disciples, which are not recorded in this book. But these are written that you may believe that Jesus is the Messiah, the Son of God, and that by believing you may have life in his name.
>
> *John 20:30–31*

John also begins his Gospel with this powerful statement about Jesus as God:

> In the beginning was the Word, and the Word was with God, and the Word was God. He was with God in the beginning. Through him all things were made; without him nothing was made that has been made. In him was life, and that life was the light of all mankind. The light shines in the darkness, and the darkness has not overcome it.
>
> There was a man sent from God whose name was John. He came as a witness to testify concerning that light, so that through him all might believe. He himself was not the light; he came only as a witness to the light.
>
> The true light that gives light to everyone was coming into the world. He was in the world, and though the world was made through him, the world did not recognize him. He came to that which was his own, but his own did not receive him. Yet to all who did receive him, to those who believed in his name, he gave the right to become children of God—children born not of natural descent, nor of human decision or a husband's will, but born of God.
>
> The Word became flesh and made his dwelling among us. We have seen his glory, the glory of the one and only Son, who came from the Father, full of grace and truth.
>
> *John 1:1–14*

Take a moment to read the passage one more time, this time circling words or phrases that speak to the deity of Christ.

Note that throughout John's Gospel, we see a strong emphasis on the signs Jesus performed in the presence of his disciples. Each of those signs are what we would call a *miracle*, and those miracles demonstrated a power that could only belong to God:

- Turning the water into wine: power over quality
- Healing the nobleman's son: power over distance
- Feeding the five thousand: power over quantity
- Walking on the water: power over nature
- Healing the man born blind: power over time
- Raising Lazarus from the dead: power over death

It's an impressive list, wouldn't you say? The following chart lists the references for the miracles that Christ performs in John's Gospel. In the right column, write down how each miracle relates to Jesus as God, based on your own personal understanding of the text.

Reference	How Jesus' Deity Is Communicated
John 1:1	
John 4:46–54	
John 6:1–14	

John 6:15–21	Jesus ~~can~~ is everywhere @ all times —
John 9:1–41	
John 11:1–44	

Write down a few sentences putting into words how you think and feel after completing your investigation. Does this strengthen or weaken your faith? Were you aware there were so many references to the deity of Christ in that one book of the New Testament? Would you be interested in completing a similar kind of study in the Gospels of Matthew, Mark, and Luke?

Put It into Practice

During this week's teaching, you saw how the virgin birth means there was a combination of both human and divine influence in Jesus. His humanity is evident in that he was born of a human mother, and his deity is evident in that he was conceived by the Holy Spirit. Jesus came as a humble servant (see Philippians 2:7) but also as a king (see John 18:36–37). Matthew's account of Jesus' birth includes a story of magi from the East who recognized Christ's kingly status. In his classic work *The Life and Times of Jesus the Messiah*, first published in 1883, Alfred Edersheim sheds light on these individuals and the gifts they brought of gold, frankincense, and myrrh:

> When taken as gifts for a newborn king, the items that the Magi brought appear inappropriate, especially the frankincense and myrrh. Gold fits the idea of kingly wealth, but perfumes would not have met the same standard.
>
> We must, instead, imagine the gifts as offerings of foreign dignitaries. Just as diplomats from other countries often bring gifts representing their cultures, these magi brought the products specific to theirs. They honored the King of the Jews in a way that fit their nationality. In this way, in fact, they stood in as representatives of all the non-Jewish nations. Their acknowledgement presaged the offer of grace to all peoples of the earth, and their gifts hinted at the coming of Gentiles to offer themselves to Christ.
>
> The ancient church also understood the gifts to symbolize aspects of Christ's life and ministry, the work He would do. The gold . . . suggested His royalty as King of the Jews and Lord of lords. In the frankincense, they saw His divinity. The myrrh

> represented His humanity—and that to the fullest extent because myrrh suggests death and burial. Thus, the gifts came to show Jesus as King, God, and Man.

Ask children what they would like for Christmas, and before you know it they will have produced *a list* of the gifts they want to receive. Today, turn the tables on that custom. In the space below, create a list of gifts you want to *give* to Jesus this Christmas. A helpful way to think about this is by using three sub-points for your gifts—your time, your talent, and your treasure.

Time

I will volunteer for . . . OCC

I will join my church for these activities . . .

find a church

I will do this to spend more time reading my Bible . . .

Join Bible Study

Talent

The things I feel I do well are . . .

Lead -

The things others say I do well are . . .

Care & Compassion

I will use these talents to . . .

to become pt advocate

Treasure

I will donate money to . . .

OCC - others in need

I will do these things anonymously to help those in need . . .

help people who need

I will support my church regularly by . . .

With these items related to your time, you talent, and your treasure in mind, write out your Christmas gift list for Jesus:

This year, I will give Jesus . . .

my all in all He has me do-

Don't forget to check in with your partner this week! See what that person has been up to and what he or she has been learning. You may want to share with each other your Christmas gift list. In what ways are your lists similar? How are they different? Get up to date on each other's prayer requests before your conversation concludes.

CLOSING REFLECTION

"Personally, I think a lot of Christians—even conservative, Bible-believing Christians—are semi-docetic."

The comment from scholar Craig A. Evans took me off-guard. I was interviewing him in his colonial-style house in a heavily wooded community near Acadia University, where he serves as a professor of New Testament. Evans had come to Acadia University in 2002 after spending more than twenty years as a professor at Trinity Western University, where he directed the graduate programs in biblical studies and founded the Dead Sea Scrolls Institute.

"What do you mean?" I asked.

"In other words," he said, "they halfway believe—without ever giving it any serious thought—what the Docetic Gnostics believed, which is that Jesus actually wasn't real. 'Oh, yes, of course, he's real,' they'll say. But they're not entirely sure how far to go with the incarnation. How *human* was Jesus? For a lot of them, the human side of Jesus is superficial.

"It's almost as though a lot of Christians think of Jesus as God wearing a human mask. He's sort of faking it, pretending to be human. He pretends to perspire, his stomach only appears to gurgle because, of course, he's not really hungry.

In fact, he doesn't really need to eat. So Jesus is the bionic Son of God who isn't really human. This is thought to be an exalted Christology, but it's not. Orthodox Christology also embraces fully the humanity of Jesus.

"What I'm saying is that the divine nature of Jesus should never militate against his full humanity. When that part gets lost, you end up with a pretty superficial understanding of Christology. For example, could Jesus read? 'Of course he could read! He's the Son of God!' That's not a good answer. At the age of three days, was Jesus fluent in Hebrew? Could he do quantum physics? Well, then, why does the book of Hebrews talk about him learning and so forth?"

I was listening intently. "So we miss his humanity," I said, half to myself and half to Evans.

"Yeah, we do," he said. "We find ourselves fussing and fuming over the divinity, but we miss the humanity. And from the historic point of view of the early church, that's just as serious an error as, say, the Ebionite direction, which was to deny the divinity."

Wanting him to explain further, I asked, "What is it we miss about his humanity?"

"Well, a big part of the atonement. He dies in our place as a human being. God didn't send an angel," he replied. "And, of course, there's the identification factor. We can identify with him: he was tempted as we are. How was he tempted if he was just God wearing a mask—faking it and pretending to be a human? Again, that's Docetic Gnosticism—Jesus only appeared to be incarnate, only appeared to be human—and a lot of evangelical Christians come pretty close to that."

"Is there something about his human nature you'd want to emphasize?"

Evans reflected for a moment, then replied. "Yes, Jesus' own faith," he said. "He tells his disciples to have faith. Jesus has a huge amount of credibility if we see him as fully human and he actually, as a human, has faith in God. Otherwise, well, that's easy for him to say! Good grief—he's been in heaven, and now he's walking around telling me to have faith? But I take the teaching of Jesus' humanness, which is taught clearly in Scripture, very seriously."

–*Lee Strobel, from* In Defense of Jesus

SESSION 4

The Prophetic Fingerprint

• • • • • • • • •

We could cope—the world could cope—with a Jesus who ultimately remains a wonderful idea inside his disciples' minds and hearts. The world cannot cope with a Jesus . . . who inaugurates God's new creation right in the middle of the old one.

–N. T. Wright, *Surprised by Hope*

Introduction

What do Jim Carrey, George C. Scott, Albert Finney, Tim Curry, Kelsey Grammer, Patrick Stewart, Michael Caine, Walter Matthau, Alastair Sim, and Scrooge McDuck all have in common? I'll give you a hint—they all relate to the year 1843.

Did you figure it out? All of these have taken on the role of Ebenezer Scrooge, the main character in Charles Dickens's classic tale *A Christmas Carol*. First published in 1843, it's safe to say Dickens never imagined his story would be performed in theater, on radio, on television, and in the movies. And not just with live actors. Ebenezer Scrooge has found success as an animated cartoon character, being played by such luminaries as Scrooge McDuck, Yosemite Sam, Fred Flintstone, and Mr. Magoo.

Attempting to determine which human actor played the best Ebenezer Scrooge is as perilous as trying to determine which human actor played the best James Bond—everyone has their favorite. All the movie adaptations put their own spin on the classic tale. But the primary plotline remains the same: the transformation of the story's main character, Scrooge.

So many people have attempted to describe Scrooge, but the best description comes from Dickens himself: "He was a tight-fisted hand at the grindstone . . . a squeezing, wrenching, grasping, scraping, clutching, covetous old sinner!" Early on in the story, we see his absolute contempt for Christmas. In one heated exchange with his nephew, he says:

> If I could work my will . . . every idiot who goes about with "Merry Christmas" on his lips should be boiled with his own pudding, and buried with a stake of holly through his heart. He should!

This leads to famous visits from three ghosts—Christmas Past, Christmas Present, and Christmas Future—who ultimately produce the desired effect on old Scrooge. By the end of the tale, the result is a new and changed man:

> Scrooge was better than his word. . . . He became as good a friend, as good a master, as good a man as the good old city knew, or any other good old city, town, or borough in the good old world. Some people laughed to see the alteration in him, but he let them laugh, and little heeded them; for he was wise enough to know that nothing ever happened on this globe, for good, at which some people did not have their fill of laughter at the outset.

The message of the gospel is that because Jesus came to this world, we can also become new creations (see 2 Corinthians 2:17). When sin entered the world in the Garden of Eden, it separated us from God. But God, in his mercy, promised to send a Savior to restore the relationship. As the Lord declared through the prophet Isaiah, "The Redeemer will come to Zion, to those in Jacob who repent of their sins" (Isaiah 59:20).

The Old Testament writers made numerous other references to the coming of this Messiah who would free God's people from their sins. The Old Testament is filled with these biographical statements, called prophecies, that serve like a modern fingerprint to identify this person. And as we will see in this session, *only Jesus* matched this precise prophetic fingerprint.

Before You Watch

If there's a group member you haven't yet partnered with for this section, get together and talk about the following questions:

- How many times would you guess you've watched *A Christmas Carol*? Which is your favorite version? Why?
- Who is your favorite actor to play the part of Ebenezer Scrooge? What is it about this actor's performance that makes it your favorite?
- Why do you think there have been so many adaptations and retellings of *A Christmas Carol*? What about the story do you think most resonates with people?

Video Teaching

Play the video segment for session four. As you watch, use the following outline to record any thoughts or concepts that stand out to you.

Notes

The Bible's prophecies about the coming of the Messiah lead us not only to the place where he would be born but to the very individual himself. In the end, only the baby in the manger can be pinpointed as the one-and-only Messiah and Son of God.

The prophet Micah had foretold the birthplace of the Messiah hundreds of years before the time of Christ. So when Herod asked his chief priests and teachers where the Messiah would be born, they knew the answer right away: *Bethlehem.*

Critics say Matthew was wrong when he applied Isaiah 7:4 to the birth of Jesus because the prophecy referred to King Ahaz, the word *virgin* was a mistranslation, and Jesus was not named Immanuel. But delving into this controversy, we find:

First, there was a broader messianic context that remained unfulfilled.

Second, there was no one word in biblical Hebrews that only meant *virgin.*

Third, biblical names are often symbolic—Jesus *is* Immanuel.

Billions of people have lived in history. But only Jesus managed to fulfill the dozens of ancient prophecies required to be the Messiah.

The real purpose of Christmas is Easter. Through Jesus' atoning death on the cross, he paid for our sins so the doors of heaven could be flung open wide for us.

As Dr. Michael Brown concluded, "What sacrifice is great enough to cover the guilt of the entire world? Who's pure enough? Who's perfect enough? Only this one, the great Son of God."

Paul captures it so well in Philippians 2:6–11 when he describes the wonder and beauty and power of the incarnation. Perhaps, in a sense, it was even the very first Christmas carol!

Group Discussion

Once the video has concluded, break up into small groups for a final time of discussion. Once again, try to get with the same people you have been meeting with for the past sessions.

1. In general, how would you describe the relationship between the Old Testament and the New Testament? How important is it that the Old Testament prophecies concerning the Messiah are fulfilled in Jesus in the New Testament?

   Extremely important to show it is a true prophecy or happening & not just a story

2. Read aloud Philippians 2:1–11. What strikes you as you hear this description of Christ humbling himself? What does the passage mean to you personally?

   To not brag or boast - give Christ & others all credit

3. How do you respond to the idea that "the real purpose of Christmas is Easter"? How do you connect the two holidays in your life? What advice would you give someone who doesn't see the connection between them?

   Christ had to be born as a human in order to die on the cross to fulfill the prophecy of forgiving our sins

4. What has this four-week study meant to you? What are two or three things you've learned as a result of this time together? For what questions did you get answers? What unanswered questions are still rolling around in your mind?

Just re-confirmed my belief that Christ was actually human-born of the Virgin Mary - so He could die for our sins

Closing Prayer

Take a few moments for one final session of prayer. Thank the Lord for the answers he has delivered to your group during the past few weeks and continue to ask him for the ones that continue to be unanswered. If appropriate, share your contact information with the other group members so you can all remain connected even after this study has concluded.

SESSION 4

Final Personal Study

Reflect on the content you've covered this final week by engaging in any or all of the following personal study. Think about what you've learned during this study and how it has strengthened your faith in the story of Jesus' birth as told in the Gospels. The time you invest in this last time of study will be well spent, so let God use it to draw you closer to him.

Study God's Word

There are dozens of prophecies in the Old Testament concerning the Messiah that could only be fulfilled by Jesus. The following are just a few for you to read and consider:

> I will put enmity between you and the woman, and between your offspring and hers; he will crush your head, and you will strike his heel.
>
> *Genesis 3:15*

I am poured out like water, and all my bones are out of joint. My heart has turned to wax; it has melted within me. My mouth is dried up like a potsherd, and my tongue sticks to the roof of my mouth; you lay me in the dust of death. Dogs surround me, a pack of villains encircles me; they pierce my hands and my feet. All my bones are on display; people stare and gloat over me. They divide my clothes among them and cast lots for my garment.

Psalm 22:14–18

Therefore the Lord himself will give you a sign: The virgin will conceive and give birth to a son, and will call him Immanuel.

Isaiah 7:14

For to us a child is born, to us a son is given, and the government will be on his shoulders. And he will be called Wonderful Counselor, Mighty God, Everlasting Father, Prince of Peace. Of the greatness of his government and peace there will be no end. He will reign on David's throne and over his kingdom, establishing and upholding it with justice and righteousness from that time on and forever. The zeal of the LORD Almighty will accomplish this.

Isaiah 9:6–7

A voice of one calling: "In the wilderness prepare the way for the LORD; make straight in the desert a highway for our God. Every valley shall be raised up, every mountain and hill made low; the rough ground shall become level, the rugged places a plain. And the glory of the LORD will be revealed, and all people will see it together. For the mouth of the LORD has spoken."

Isaiah 40:3–5

When Israel was a child, I loved him, and out of Egypt I called my son.

Hosea 11:1

But you, Bethlehem Ephrathah, though you are small among the clans of Judah, out of you will come for me one who will be ruler over Israel, whose origins are from of old, from ancient times.

Micah 5:2

Rejoice greatly, Daughter Zion! Shout, Daughter Jerusalem! See, your king comes to you, righteous and victorious, lowly and riding on a donkey, on a colt, the foal of a donkey.

Zechariah 9:9

I told them, "If you think it best, give me my pay; but if not, keep it." So they paid me thirty pieces of silver. And the LORD said to me, "Throw it to the potter"—the handsome price at which they valued me! So I took the thirty pieces of silver and threw them to the potter at the house of the LORD.

Zechariah 11:12–13

See, I will send the prophet Elijah to you before that great and dreadful day of the LORD comes. He will turn the hearts of the parents to their children, and the hearts of the children to their parents; or else I will come and strike the land with total destruction.

Malachi 4:5–6

Each of the prophecies you just read, and its corresponding fulfillment in Christ, are listed in the left-hand column of the following table. In the center column, write a summary of the prophecy.

In the right column, write why you feel it has a special importance. (Note there are no right or wrong comments here—this is all about what the Lord is saying to you personally.)

Prophecy / ***Fulfillment***	**Summary of Prophecy**	**Why It Is Important to You**
Genesis 3:15 / *1 John 3:8*		
Psalm 22:14–18 / *John 19:23–37*	What took place on the cross	Fulfilment of God sending His only son to die for our sins
Isaiah 7:14 / *Luke 1:35*	Immaculate conception	One of the most important steps
Isaiah 9:6–7 / *Luke 1:32–33*		
Isaiah 40:3–5 / *John 1:23*		
Hosea 11:1 / *Matthew 2:14–15*		
Micah 5:2 / *Matthew 2:4–6*		
Zechariah 9:9 / *Matthew 21:8–10*		
Zechariah 11:12–13 /*Matthew 27:6–10*		
Malachi 4:5–6 / *Matthew 11:10–15*		

Put It into Practice

Letter writing is a lost art in our day and age. Thanks to emails and texts, we've reduced everything to brief phrases and short sentences. During the past few weeks, you have explored many things related to the birth of Christ. You've also been encouraged to reach out and communicate some of what you've learned and discovered with someone else.

In that spirit, take some time to write a letter. The letter can be to someone imaginary, but it would be more effective to write it to a real person who would benefit from hearing what you've learned. Perhaps it's a family member or an old friend. Or maybe it's a neighbor or a coworker. As you went through *The Case for Christmas* study, the Lord has undoubtedly brought some person to mind with whom you would like to share this information.

Page back through this study guide and make a short list of four or five things that stood out to you. Use those points as your outline for the letter (see the page provided). End with an invitation for the person to respond if he or she wants to go deeper with you about the true story of Christmas.

Point 1:

Point 2:

Point 3:

Point 4:

Point 5:

When you finish the first letter, then write a letter to God, using the page provided. Express how you feel about the true meaning of Christmas and communicate your gratitude for what the real message of Christmas is all about. Once again, you may find it helpful to go back through this study guide and look for nuggets of truth you highlighted in your notes. Thank the Lord for not only what he accomplished at Christmas but also what he accomplished at Easter. Share your personal spiritual condition with him and ask him to help you get the answers to the questions that still remain. He will help you.

Dear ______________________________:

Dear Lord,

Thank you for sending
Your only son to be born
of the Virgin Mary - to
fulfill the prophecy that
you promised - Jesus
came as a human
to die on the Cross to
forgive us our sins -
Please help non-believers
to open their hearts to
accept you as their
Savior -
Amen

CLOSING REFLECTION

After spending nearly two years investigating the identity of the Christmas child, I was ready to reach a verdict. For me, the evidence was clear and compelling. Yes, Christmas is a holiday overlaid with all sorts of fanciful beliefs from flying reindeer to Santa Claus sliding down chimneys. But I became convinced that if you drill down to its core, Christmas is based on a historical reality—the incarnation: God becoming man, Spirit taking on flesh, the infinite entering the finite, the eternal becoming time-bound. It's a mystery backed up by facts that I now believed were simply too strong to ignore.

I had come to the point where I was ready for the Christmas gift that Perfecta Delgado had told me about years earlier: the Christ child, whose love and grace are offered freely to everyone who receives him in repentance and faith. Even someone like me.

So I talked to God in a heartfelt and unedited prayer, admitting and turning from my wrongdoing, and receiving his offer of forgiveness and eternal life through Jesus. I told him that with his help I wanted to follow him and his ways from here on out.

There was no choir of heavenly angels, no lightning bolts, no tingly sensations, no audible reply. I know that some people feel a rush of emotion at such a moment; as for me there was something else that was equally exhilarating: there was a rush of reason.

Over time, however, there has been so much more. As I have endeavored to follow Jesus' teaching and open myself to his transforming power, my priorities, my values, my character, my worldview, my attitudes, and my relationships have been changing—for the better. It has been a humbling affirmation of the apostle Paul's words: "Therefore if anyone is in Christ, he is a new creation; the old is gone, the new has come."

And now, what about you?

Perhaps, like the first-century sheepherders, your next step should be to further investigate the evidence for yourself. You need to get answers to the spiritual sticking points that are keeping you from following Jesus. It's my hope that you'll promise yourself at the outset that when the facts are in, you'll reach your own verdict in the case for Christmas.

Or maybe you're more like the magi. Through a series of circumstances, including the reading of this book, you've maneuvered your way through the hoopla and glitter and distractions of the holiday season, and now you've finally come into the presence of the baby who was born to change your life and rewrite your eternal destination.

Go ahead, talk to him. Offer your worship and your life. And let him give you what Perfecta Delgado called the greatest gift of all.

Himself.

–*Lee Strobel, from* The Case for Christmas

Leader's Guide

Thank you for your willingness to lead your group through this study! What you have chosen to do is valuable and will make a great difference in the lives of others. The rewards of being a leader are different from those who are participating, and we hope that as you lead you will find your own walk with Jesus deepened by this experience.

The Case for Christmas is a four-session study built around video content and small-group interaction. As the group leader, think of yourself as the host. Your job is to take care of your guests by managing the behind-the-scenes details so that when everyone arrives, they can enjoy their time together. As the leader, your role is not to answer all the questions or reteach the content—the video, book, and study guide will do that work. Your job is to guide the experience and cultivate your small group into a kind of teaching community. This will make it a place for members to process, question, and reflect—not receive more instruction.

Before your first meeting, make sure everyone in the group gets a copy of the study guide. This will keep everyone on the same page and help the process run more smoothly. If some group members are unable to purchase the guide, arrange it so that people can share the resource with other group members. Giving everyone access to all the material will position this study to be as rewarding an experience as possible. Everyone should feel free to write in his or her study guide and bring it to group every week.

Setting Up the Group

You will need to determine with your group how long you want to meet each week so you can plan your time accordingly. Generally, most groups like to meet from one to two hours, so you could use one of the following schedules:

Section	60 minutes	90 minutes	120 minutes
Introduction (members arrive)	5 minutes	5 minutes	10 minutes
Before You Watch (discuss the icebreaker questions as directed)	10 minutes	15 minutes	15 minutes
Video Teaching (watch the video teaching material together and take notes)	15 minutes	15 minutes	15 minutes
Group Discussion (discuss the Bible study questions you selected)	25 minutes	40 minutes	60 minutes
Closing Prayer (reflect on the takeaways, pray together, and dismiss)	5 minutes	15 minutes	20 minutes

As the group leader, you will want to create an environment that encourages sharing and learning. A church sanctuary or formal classroom may not be as ideal as a living room, because those locations can feel formal and less intimate. No matter what setting you choose, provide enough comfortable seating for everyone, and, if possible, arrange the seats in a semicircle so everyone can see the video easily. This will make transition between the video and group conversation more efficient and natural.

Also, try to get to the meeting site early so you can greet participants as they arrive. Simple refreshments create a welcoming atmosphere and can be a wonderful addition to a group study evening. Try to take food and pet allergies into account to make your guests as comfortable as possible. You may also want to consider offering childcare to couples with children who want to attend. Finally, be sure your media technology is working properly. Managing these details up front will make the rest of your group experience flow smoothly and provide a welcoming space in which to engage the content of *The Case for Christmas.*

Starting the Group Time

Once everyone has arrived, it is time to begin the group. Here are some simple tips to make your group time healthy, enjoyable, and effective.

Begin the meeting with a short prayer and remind the group members to put their phones on silent. This is a way to make sure you can all be present with one another and with God. Next, facilitate the "Before You Watch" icebreaker questions, using the directions provided in the study guide. This won't require as much time in session one, but beginning in session two, you may need more time if people also want to share any insights from their personal studies.

Leading the Discussion Time

Now that the group is engaged, watch the video and respond with some directed small-group discussion. Encourage the group members to participate in the discussion, but make sure they know they don't have to do so. As the discussion progresses, follow up with comments such as, "Tell me more about that," or, "Why did you answer that way?" This will allow the group participants to deepen their reflections and invite meaningful sharing in a nonthreatening way.

Although there are only four discussion questions for each session, you do not have to use them all or even follow them in order. Feel free to pick and choose questions based on either the needs of your group or how the conversation is flowing. Also, don't be afraid of silence. Offering a question and allowing up to thirty seconds of silence is okay. It allows people space to think about how they want to respond and also gives them time to do so.

As group leader, you are the boundary keeper for your group. Do not let anyone (yourself included) dominate the group time. Keep an eye out for group members who might be tempted to "attack" folks they disagree with or try to "fix" those having struggles. These kinds of behaviors can derail a group's momentum, so they need to be steered in a different direction. Model active listening and encourage everyone in your group to do the same. This will make your group time a safe space and create a positive community.

The group discussion leads to a closing time of reflection and prayer. During this time, encourage the participants to review what they have learned and share any needs they have with the group. Close your time by taking a few minutes to pray for those needs and to thank God for sending his Son, Jesus, into the world. The group members may also want to share requests they want the other members to pray about during the week. Beginning in session two, be sure to check in regarding these requests and see how God has answered them.

At the end of each session, invite the group members to complete the between-sessions personal study for that week. If you so choose, explain you will provide some time before the video teaching next week for anyone to share insights. Let them know sharing is optional, and it's not a problem if they can't get to the between-sessions activities some weeks. It will still be beneficial for them to hear from the other participants and learn about what they discovered.

Thank you again for taking the time to lead your group. You are making a difference in the lives of others and having an impact on the kingdom of God.

THE
CASE
FOR
CHRISTMAS
A Journalist Investigates the Identity of the Child in the Manger
LEE STROBEL

ZONDERVAN®

The Case for Easter

A Journalist Investigates the Evidence for the Resurrection

Lee Strobel
New York Times Bestselling Author

Did Jesus of Nazareth really rise from the dead?

Of the many world religions, only one claims that its founder returned from the grave. The resurrection of Jesus Christ is the very cornerstone of Christianity.

But a dead man coming back to life? In our sophisticated age, when myth has given way to science, who can take such a claim seriously? Some argue that Jesus never died on the cross. Conflicting accounts make the empty tomb seem suspect.

How credible is the evidence for—and against—the resurrection? Focusing his award-winning skills as a legal journalist on history's most compelling enigma, Lee Strobel retraces the startling findings that led him from atheism to belief. He examines:

- The Medical Evidence—Was Jesus' death a sham and his resurrection a hoax?
- The Evidence of the Missing Body—Was Jesus' body really absent from his tomb?
- The Evidence of Appearances—Was Jesus seen alive after his death on the cross?

Written in a hard-hitting journalistic style, *The Case for Easter* probes the core issues of the resurrection. Jesus Christ, risen from the dead: superstitious myth or life-changing reality? The evidence is in. The verdict is up to you.

Available in stores and online!

The Case for Miracles

A Journalist Investigates Evidence for the Supernatural

Lee Strobel

New York Times Bestselling Author

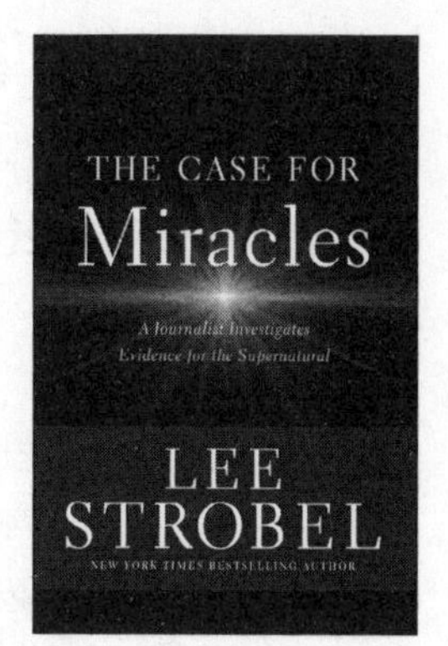

New York Times bestselling author Lee Strobel trains his investigative sights on the hot-button issue of whether it's credible to believe God intervenes supernaturally in people's lives today.

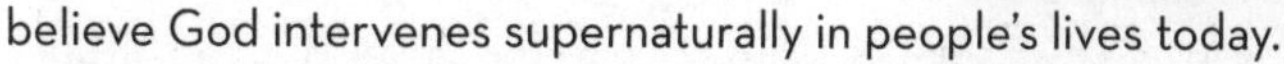

This provocative book starts with an unlikely interview in which America's foremost skeptic builds a seemingly persuasive case *against* the miraculous. But then Strobel travels the country to quiz scholars to see whether they can offer solid answers to atheist objections. Along the way, he encounters astounding accounts of healings and other phenomena that simply cannot be explained away by naturalistic causes. The book features the results of exclusive new scientific polling that shows miracle accounts are much more common than people think.

What's more, Strobel delves into the most controversial question of all: what about miracles that *don't* happen? If God *can* intervene in the world, why doesn't he do it more often to relieve suffering? Many American Christians are embarrassed by the supernatural, not wanting to look odd or extreme to their neighbors. Yet, *The Case for Miracles* shows not only that the miraculous is possible but that God still does intervene in our world in awe-inspiring ways. Here's a unique book that examines all sides of this issue and comes away with a passionate defense for God's divine action in lives today.

Available in stores and online!

The Case for Christ

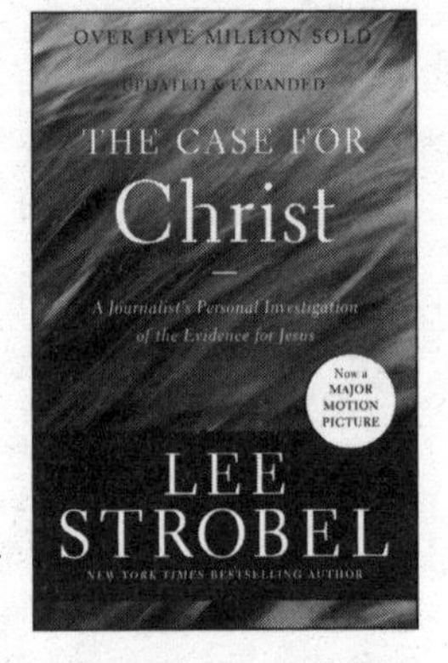

A Journalist's Personal Investigation of the Evidence for Jesus

Lee Strobel

New York Times Bestselling Author

Is there credible evidence that Jesus of Nazareth really is the Son of God?

Retracing his own spiritual journey from atheism to faith, Lee Strobel, former legal editor of the *Chicago Tribune*, cross-examines a dozen experts with doctorates from schools like Cambridge, Princeton, and Brandeis who are recognized authorities in their own fields.

Strobel challenges them with questions like: How reliable is the New Testament? Does evidence for Jesus exist outside the Bible? Is there any reason to believe the resurrection was an actual event?

Winner of the Gold Medallion Book Award and twice nominated for the Christian Book of the Year Award, Strobel's tough, point-blank questions read like a captivating, fast-paced novel. But it's not fiction. It's a riveting quest for the truth about history's most compelling figure.

The new edition includes scores of revisions and additions, including updated material on archaeological and manuscript discoveries, fresh recommendations for further study, and an interview with the author, who tells dramatic stories about the book's impact, provides behind-the-scenes information, and responds to critiques of the book by skeptics. As *The Case for Christ* and its ancillary resources approach 10 million copies in print, this updated edition will prove even more valuable to contemporary readers.

Video Curriculum Also Available!

Available in stores and online!